ASTIAN BEAR-McCLARD · VIJA CELMINS · DAVID CLAERBOUT · JENNIFER COATES · GREGORY
WDSON · SUSAN CRILE · RUSSELL CROTTY · TIM DAVIS · JEN DeNIKE · STAN DOUGLAS · JULIA
CH · SPENCER FINCH · EWAN GIBBS · SUSAN GRAHAM · LAURENT GRASSO · NEIL GUST · DAVI
MMONS · TODD HIDO · YVONNE JACQUETTE · YEON JIN KIM · HALINA KLIEM · DOINA KRAAL
NEY KULOK · CHARLES LaBELLE · CLAUDE LÉVÊQUE · ROBERT LONGO · BRITTA LUMER · VE
TER · FLORIAN MAIER-AICHEN · VIK MUNIZ · LAUREN ORCHOWSKI · JOHN PILSON · THOMA
F · PAT STEIR · DEBORAH STRATMAN · MARC SWANSON · SUSANNA THORNTON · JEFF WALL
DY WARHOL · THOMAS WEAVER · SHIZUKA YOKOMIZO · KOHEI YO...... · JOHN ZURIER
R-McCLARD · VIJA CELMINS · DAVID CLAERBOUT · JENNIFER C...... ORY CREWDSON
AN CRILE · RUSSELL CROTTY · TIM DAVIS · JEN DeNIKE · ...... NE EIRICH · S
CH · EWAN GIBBS · SUSAN GRAHAM · LAURENT GRASSO · ...... HAMMONS · TOI
O · YVONNE JACQUETTE · YEON JIN KIM · HALINA KLIEM · ...... AAL · BARNEY KULOK
ELLE · CLAUDE LÉVÊQUE · ROBERT LONGO · BRITTA LUME...... ERA LUTTER · FLORIAN MAIE
MUNIZ · LAUREN ORCHOWSKI · JOHN PILSON · THOMAS RUFF · PAT STEIR · DEBORAH STRA
RC SWANSON · SUSANNA THORNTON · JEFF WALL · ANDY WARHOL · THOMAS WEAVER · SHIZ
KOMIZO · KOHEI YOSHIYUKI · JOHN ZURIER · SEBASTIAN BEAR-McCLARD · VIJA CELMINS · DA
ERBOUT · JENNIFER COATES · GREGORY CREWDSON · SUSAN CRILE · RUSSELL CROTTY · TIM
DeNIKE · STAN DOUGLAS · JULIANE EIRICH · SPENCER FINCH · EWAN GIBBS · SUSAN GRAHAM
RENT GRASSO · NEIL GUST · DAVID HAMMONS · TODD HIDO · YVONNE JACQUETTE · YEON J
INA KLIEM · DOINA KRAAL · BARNEY KULOK · CHARLES LaBELLE · CLAUDE LÉVÊQUE · ROB
NGO · BRITTA LUMER · VERA LUTTER · FLORIAN MAIER-AICHEN · VIK MUNIZ · LAUREN ORCH
N PILSON · THOMAS RUFF · PAT STEIR · DEBORAH STRATMAN · MARC SWANSON · SUSANNA T
F WALL · ANDY WARHOL · THOMAS WEAVER · SHIZUKA YOKOMIZO · KOHEI YOSHIYUKI · JOH
ASTIAN BEAR-McCLARD · VIJA CELMINS · DAVID CLAERBOUT · JENNIFER COATES · GREGORY
EWDSON · SUSAN CRILE · RUSSELL CROTTY · TIM DAVIS · JEN DeNIKE · STAN DOUGLAS · JULIA
NCER FINCH · EWAN GIBBS · SUSAN GRAHAM · LAURENT GRASSO · NEIL GUST · DAVID HAMM
DO · YVONNE JACQUETTE · YEON JIN KIM · HALINA KLIEM · DOINA KRAAL · BARNEY KULOK
ELLE · CLAUDE LÉVÊQUE · ROBERT LONGO · BRITTA LUMER · VERA LUTTER · FLORIAN MAIE
MUNIZ · LAUREN ORCHOWSKI · JOHN PILSON · THOMAS RUFF · PAT STEIR · DEBORAH STRA
RC SWANSON · SUSANNA THORNTON · JEFF WALL · ANDY WARHOL · THOMAS WEAVER · SHIZ
KOMIZO · KOHEI YOSHIYUKI · JOHN ZURIER · SEBASTIAN BEAR-McCLARD · VIJA CELMINS · DA
ERBOUT · JENNIFER COATES · GREGORY CREWDSON · SUSAN CRILE · RUSSELL CROTTY · TIM
DeNIKE · STAN DOUGLAS · JULIANE EIRICH · SPENCER FINCH · EWAN GIBBS · SUSAN GRAHAM
RENT GRASSO · NEIL GUST · DAVID HAMMONS · TODD HIDO · YVONNE JACQUETTE · YEON J
HALINA KLIEM · DOINA KRAAL · BARNEY KULOK · CHARLES LaBELLE · CLAUDE LÉVÊQUE
BERT LONGO · BRITTA LUMER · VERA LUTTER · FLORIAN MAIER-AICHEN · VIK MUNIZ · LAUR
CHOWSKI · JOHN PILSON · THOMAS RUFF · PAT STEIR · DEBORAH STRATMAN · MARC SWANSO
SANNA THORNTON · JEFF WALL · ANDY WARHOL · THOMAS WEAVER · SHIZUKA YOKOMIZO
SHIYUKI · JOHN ZURIER · SEBASTIAN BEAR-McCLARD · VIJA CELMINS · to:Night · DAVID CLAER
UT · JENNIFER COATES · **CONTEMPORARY REPRESENTATIONS OF THE NIGHT** · GREGORY CR
SAN CRILE · RUSSELL CROTTY · TIM DAVIS · JEN DeNIKE · STAN DOUGLAS · JULIANE EIRICH
CH · EWAN GIBBS · SUSAN GRAHAM · LAURENT GRASSO · NEIL GUST · DAVID HAMMONS · TOI
ONNE JACQUETTE · YEON JIN KIM · HALINA KLIEM · DOINA KRAAL · BARNEY KULOK · CHAR
UDE LÉVÊQUE · ROBERT LONGO · BRITTA LUMER · VERA LUTTER · FLORIAN MAIER

to : Night

WE WOULD LIKE TO GIVE SPECIAL THANKS TO
DR. SUSAN ('75) & DAVID BERSHAD FOR THEIR
CONTINUED SUPPORT OF THE HUNTER COLLEGE
ART GALLERIES.

to : Night

CONTEMPORARY
REPRESENTATIONS
OF THE NIGHT

Curated by Joachim Pissarro,
Mara Hoberman & Julia Moreno

THE HUNTER COLLEGE ART GALLERIES

THE BERTHA AND KARL LEUBSDORF ART GALLERY
SEPTEMBER 25 - DECEMBER 6, 2008

TIMES SQUARE GALLERY
SEPTEMBER 25 - NOVEMBER 15, 2008

CONTENTS

PRESIDENT'S FOREWORD

On behalf of Hunter College, I welcome you to the exhibition "to: Night: Contemporary Representations of the Night." This project is presented in tandem with the Museum of Modern Art's "Van Gogh and the Colors of the Night," curated by Joachim Pissarro, Bershad Professor of Art History and Director of the Hunter College Art Galleries. We are grateful to Professor Pissarro and his outstanding co-curators on this project, Mara Hoberman and Julia Moreno, for bringing together these important 21st-century perspectives on the van Gogh paintings exhibited at the MoMA.

Hunter's galleries and art department have been a vital part of the New York cultural landscape for decades. And for the next few months, this is quite literally the case – thanks to Laurent Grasso and his *Infinite Light* sculpture that currently spans the pedestrian bridges connecting the three buildings of Hunter's main campus. By transforming Hunter's architecture into a virtual outdoor gallery, Grasso has highlighted our essential role in the life of the neighborhood, community, and city. *Infinite Light* is a celebration of the past, present, and future of this great public institution.

We are grateful to all of those whose generosity made this project possible. Thank you for joining us for this exciting and moving exhibition.

– JENNIFER J. RAAB
  PRESIDENT, HUNTER COLLEGE

PREFACE

When Gertrude Stein famously stated, "a rose is a rose is a rose," she established a position both quintessentially modern and quintessentially postmodern. By rejecting the evocative power of symbolic roses, she denied the efficacy of past tropes to account for modern experience, which is the act of a modernist. By quoting the past to prove its obsolescence, she revived or at least extended it as a point of reference, a practice said to be key to postmodernism. Let's not argue about the border between modernism and postmodernism; the issue of past tropes remains, and it is writ large across the title of this show, for night is a trove of tropes of great antiquity and widespread application. If the theme of night seems to lack specificity, though, imagine what a "to: Day" show would look like: Ubiquity would burst the bounds of specification, and no overarching theme could emerge. The night, however, is the ob-scene alternative to the day, the space in which all the passion and horror restrained by the sun are set loose. What is the contemporary artist to do with such a reservoir of ancient associations? This show is the answer, and the answer is: quite a lot.

What characterizes "to: Night" is a relation – a relation between two asymmetric things – and that relation comprises an insoluble puzzle. I am talking about the relation between night as a fixed, delimited category on the one hand, and humanity's unlimited generation of versions or representations of the abstract category on the other. Because we cannot grasp the absolute category hidden behind the word *night*, we might as well put it under erasure: ~~Night~~. The versions, however, perform an intense dance around this razed site, and we may want to ask how, and why.

The idea of versions strongly underscores the character of this exhibition, as a great range of materials, mimetic methods, and strategies of presentation constitute a flux of mediation that is highly open-ended. All these versions add up to not a contemporary concept of night, but a contemporary awareness of the contingent, fragmentary character of our representations. The range of work in "to: Night" accentuates this contingency by holding the variable versions of contemporary art practice up to this category deemed replete unto itself: night.

In the movie *Bus Stop*, Marilyn Monroe's character is a honky-tonk singer who declares her ambition to be a "chan*toos*." Her fallen relation to language is emblematic: We also aspire to be chantooses, to sing the praises of night. Here we reach the crux of our own limitations: We cannot quite capture the romance that was Night. We can only celebrate the romance of night for what it is – a feeling we cannot live without.

— THOMAS WEAVER
CHAIR, ART DEPARTMENT, HUNTER COLLEGE
EXECUTIVE DIRECTOR, HUNTER COLLEGE ART
GALLERIES

ACKNOWLEDGMENTS

As is the case with all exhibitions organized within a university art gallery, "to: Night" is the result of a rich and diverse collaboration between students, faculty, and administrative officials. In the case of this particular show, Mara Hoberman (Curator and Hunter College Art History MA, class of 2009) and Julia Moreno (Curator) took on the ambitious task of exploring a concept that has interested me (Joachim Pissarro) for quite some time and even more so since I began curating an exhibition of van Gogh's nocturnal works for The Museum of Modern Art – this exhibition project provided the stimulus for the present project. The question addressed by "to: Night" is: Were van Gogh alive today, how would he conceive of the nocturnal reality, and through what kind of media would he investigate it? Over forty artists provide elements of the answer to this particular conundrum. The research that led to the present exhibition yielded a surprisingly fecund list of artists who employed an equally surprising diversity of media and conceptual approaches. None of us could have predicted the bounty of material that my two curatorial colleagues came back with and I thank them for their impressive work in researching and realizing the "to: Night" exhibition and catalog.

Naturally, our curatorial team received ample and invaluable support from many parts of the Hunter College community. I would like to thank Jennifer J. Raab, President of Hunter College. for her tremendous enthusiasm for the "to: Night" project from its incipient point, and for making it possible to realize such a large-scale show at the Hunter College Art Galleries. I would also like to thank Jayne Rosengarten and Eve Levy for their help in providing financial support the project. Additional hearty thanks go to Rick Chandler, Conan Freud, Anne Lytle, and Elizabeth McKee for their involvement with this exhibition in every complex aspect, and, in particular, for their work on the Laurent Grasso *Infinite Light* installation on the pedestrian bridges of the main Hunter College campus at 68th Street and Lexington Avenue.

The project "to: Night" also found strong allies and support in the Art Department of Hunter College. Many thanks to Thomas Weaver, Chair of the Art Department, for his creative and administrative input, both of which helped in making the exhibition a reality. I would like to express sincere gratitude to the Hunter College Art Gallery Committee: Professors Emily Braun, Susan Crile, Jeff Mongrain, Katy Siegel, Nari Ward, and Thomas Weaver. The Gallery Committee saw the potential of this extraordinary exhibition and gave advice and support to the two young curators from beginning to end. Tracy Adler, Curator of the Hunter College Art Galleries, also deserves our heartfelt thanks for helping to facilitate the taxing aspects of the organization and implementation of the exhibition. Furthermore,

I would like to extend thanks to the entire Art Department of Hunter College, who provided a creatively stimulating environment in which good ideas never fall on deaf ears.

And last but certainly not least, I would like to express my sincere gratitude to all of the generous donors to the "to: Night" exhibition. The following people made it possible for us to bring to the Hunter College Art Galleries a full vision of contemporary representations of night. I would like to express my deepest gratitude to Marylin B. Arison for her exceedingly generous support of the exhibition and accompanying catalog from the inception of this project. "to: Night" would have never been possible without the crucial contributions of many friends. I am especially indebted to: Dr. Susan and David Bershad; Phyllis and Joseph Caroff; Charles and Jan Cowles; The Cowles Charitable Trust; The Cultural Services of the French Embassy; Bunny Dell; Fifth Floor Foundation; Glenn Fuhrman; Helene Goldfarb; Harriet Gruber; Eve Haberman; Hunter Deli; Lucille D. Kaufman; Evelyn Kranes Kossak; Phyllis L. Kossoff; Nanette Laitman; John Leubsdorf; Roz Levin; Joan Masket and Sherman Pincus; Connelly and McLaughlin; The Mondriaan Foundation; The Netherlands Foundation for Visual Arts, Design and Architecture; Pommery Champagne; The Susan and Elihu Rose Foundation; Anita Shapolsky; Alicia M. G. Siebenaler; The Ruth Stanton Foundation; The Vance Wall Foundation; and Judith and Stanley Zabar.

— JOACHIM PISSARRO
BERSHAD PROFESSOR OF ART HISTORY &
DIRECTOR OF THE HUNTER COLLEGE ART
GALLERIES

Organizing "to: Night" has been an immensely rewarding collaborative process. Many individuals helped realize this project and we hope that all who were involved are as proud as we are of the end product. As two young curators just beginning our careers, we (Mara Hoberman and Julia Moreno) are indebted to numerous seasoned professionals who helped show us the ropes and guided us through the curatorial process. First, we would like to express our deepest gratitude to Joachim Pissarro, Director of the Hunter College Art Galleries. Without his incredible dedication, brilliant ideas, and steadfast support, it would not have been possible to pull off an exhibition of this magnitude. Joachim conceived of the idea for an exhibition of contemporary representations of night and remained a constant source of inspiration throughout the planning and implementation stages, which culminated in this exciting exhibition and beautiful catalog.

We would like to express a special thank you to Jennifer J. Raab, President of Hunter College. She was a strong supporter of "to: Night" from the very beginning and her enthusiasm for such a large-scale project (including some potentially challenging art installations) was an incredible boon for the exhibition and the future of the Hunter College Art Galleries. We are extremely grateful for her unwavering confidence in this project. In addition, we would like to thank Jayne Rosengarten, Eve Levy, and Sarah Wilburn in the Institutional Advancement Department of Hunter College for their assistance with the fundraising for the "to: Night" exhibition and catalog.

Many generous donors contributed funds toward the realization of the exhibition and we would like to thank them warmly for their support: Marylin B. Arison; Dr. Susan and David Bershad; Phyllis and Joseph Caroff; Charles and Jan Cowles; The Cowles Charitable Trust; The Cultural Services of the French Embassy; Bunny Dell; Fifth Floor Foundation; Glenn Fuhrman; Helene Goldfarb; Harriet Gruber; Eve Haberman; Hunter Deli; Lucille D. Kaufman; Evelyn Kranes Kossak; Phyllis L. Kossoff; Nanette Laitman; John Leubsdorf; Roz Levin; Joan Masket and Sherman Pincus; Connelly and McLaughlin; The Mondriaan Foundation; The Netherlands Foundation for Visual Arts, Design and Architecture; Pommery Champagne; The Susan and Elihu Rose Foundation; Anita Shapolsky; Alicia M. G. Siebenaler; The Ruth Stanton Foundation; The Vance Wall Foundation; and Judith and Stanley Zabar.

We would also like to thank faculty and staff members in the Hunter College Art Department who provided encouragement and support for "to: Night." Thomas Weaver, Chair of the Art Department and Executive Director of the Hunter College Art Galleries, deserves a warm thank you for his role in making this show a reality and for his thoughtful preface in this catalog. Similarly, the members of the Hunter College Art Galleries Committee – Emily Braun, Susan Crile, Jeff Mongrain, Katy Siegel, Nari Ward, and Thomas Weaver – all provided invaluable ideas and advice that helped shape and make possible this exhibition. Additional thanks go to Katy for contributing an intelligent and original catalog essay. Tracy Adler, Curator of the Hunter College Art Galleries, was another priceless resource when planning this show. We greatly appreciate her dedicated effort on behalf of this exhibition, both creatively and pragmatically.

We feel lucky to have worked with a talented graphic design team to develop the visual identity for the "to: Night" exhibition and the catalog design. Cynthia Pratomo and Chen Chieh Ni of the C/C design firm produced beautiful work and helped bring a cohesive aesthetic identity to the exhibition. Our research assistant, Jesse White, did an amazing job compiling information on all of the artists represented in the show and we are indebted to him for his hard work and dedication to working with us on this catalog. Thank you to our terrific editor, Casey Ruble, for her work on this catalog and related exhibition texts.

We are grateful to our preparator Phi Nuygen and his crew for their supreme work readying the galleries and installing the work at both exhibition venues. We would also like to thank Tim Laun, Hunter's MFA Building Manager, for his support and assistance in realizing this project. Our registrar, Meg Krol, was a tremendous help during the final stages of the show and we are grateful for her assistance in bringing artwork from near and far to Hunter College. Thank you to Hugh Walton for advising us on the technical aspects of the exhibition. Many thanks to Birte Kleemann for sharing her wonderful suggestions and ideas with us. And thank you to our intern, Yeon Jin Kim, who provided valuable assistance toward realizing the "to: Night" exhibition and catalog.

The Laurent Grasso *Infinite Light* installation required a tremendous amount of support from many members of the Hunter community and beyond. Again, we are indebted to President Raab for her enthusiasm for this unprecedented installation of artwork on the exterior of the pedestrian bridges of the main Hunter College campus. We are grateful to Rick Chandler, Acting Vice President for Administration, and Elizabeth McKee, Acting Director of External Affairs, for guiding the *Infinite Light* project from proposal to fruition. We would also like to extend warm thanks to Giancarlo Bonagura, Ed Pearlmutter, and Andrew Silver for their assistance with this project. Conan Freud, Vice President for Administration, and

Scott Lewis, Engineer, provided essential support for the *Infinite Light* project and we are extremely grateful for their assistance. We are thrilled to have been able to work with the talented and ever-capable Jeff Friedman and Mark Cohen from LET THERE BE NEON in recreating Grasso's neon installation specifically for the bridges at Hunter College. We would also like to thank the Cultural Services of the French Embassy for sponsoring Grasso's trip to New York City to oversee the installation of *Infinite Light*.

In addition to expressing our gratitude to the artists, we would like to thank all of the galleries and collectors who contributed time and effort in order to make this exhibition possible. Special thanks go to: Kristen Becker at Luhring Augustine Gallery; Larry Becker at Larry Becker Contemporary Art; Olivier Belot, Elodie Cazes, and Cornelia Tischmacher at Yvon Lambert Gallery; Edward De Luca and Kate Pollack at DC Moore Gallery; Susan Feldman at Vera Lutter's studio; Marisol Ferradad of Soledad Senlle Art Gallery, Amsterdam; Glenn Fuhrman, Alexandra Gaty, and Renée Martin at Blum & Poe; Marian Goodman and Leslie Nolen at Marian Goodman Gallery; Sabine Gottfried at Duve Gallery, Berlin; Laurent Grasso and Joe Tang at Galerie Chez Valentin; Sandy Heller and Chloe Schon at The Heller Group; Tom Heman and James Woodward at Metro Pictures; Allison Kave and Becky Smith at Bellwether Gallery; Nicole Klagsbrun and Ruth Phaneuf at Nicole Klagsbrun Gallery; Anna Kustera at Anna Kustera Gallery; Greg Lulay and Kelly Reynolds at Zwirner and Wirth Gallery; Meg Malloy at Sikkema Jenkins & Co.; Renee McKee and Anders Bergstrom at McKee Gallery; Kamel Mennour and Jessy Mansuy-Leydier at Kamel Mennour Gallery; Greg Pierce at the Andy Warhol Museum; Liz Raizes at Greenberg Van Doren Gallery; Stephanie Roach at The Flag Art Foundation; Celene Ryan and David Stroud at Hosfelt Gallery; Alissa Schoenfeld and Anita Totha at Yossi Milo Gallery; Lisa Schroeder and Sara Jo Romero of Schroeder Romero Gallery; Amy Smith-Stewart at Smith-Stewart Gallery; Luke Stettner from Spencer Finch's studio; Kristina Sumption at Pace Prints; Putri Tan at Gagosian Gallery; Michelle Tillou at Kinz, Tillou and Feigen; and David Zwirner and Angela Choon at David Zwirner Gallery.

— MARA HOBERMAN & JULIA MORENO
CURATORS

THE NIGHT'S THOUSAND EYES

From the beginning of time, night has been an abiding subject of fascination and investigation, eliciting mystery, awe, inspiration, fear, and multifarious intermediary emotions concurrently. This exhibition, which contains approximately sixty works by over forty artists, offers a sample of the prodigious diversity of aesthetic stances that are possible today in response to one of the greatest conundrums of all time. Even if this exhibition, by its very subject, ties our present to the earliest history of mankind, contemporary representations and treatments of night, as seen here, vary vastly from pre-modern, and even modern, conceptions.

In order to highlight the particularity of today's representations of the night, it is, therefore, useful to take a short detour through a few historical precedents. One of the very first representations of night in the history of Western art appears in an exquisite medieval manuscript, the *Book of Hours of the Duke of Berry*, which was made for and commissioned by the Duke of Berry. This hand-written, hand-painted book, held today at The Cloisters in New York City, carries a particularly vivid page that represents a crucifixion and illustrates "the darkness that came upon the earth from the sixth to the ninth hour." This painted page, executed with soft-tone, hazy grays offset by a streak of flame in the sky, constitutes one of the rare and earliest representations of night in the medieval age.[2]

Beautiful and moving as it is, this representation of the night has almost nothing to do with our perceptions of the nocturnal world today. In the manuscript page, night's darkness appears to be a metaphor, or rather a recurrent signal of death – specifically, the death of all deaths: that of the One who sacrificed himself for mankind. The night, therefore, was never experienced in itself, but rather as an unavoidable phenomenon that carried within it the very essence of the relationship between God and mankind: God sacrificed himself (at which point night came upon us) before resurrection, redemption, and the promise of eternal life (symbolized on that page by a streak of flame) opened up a brighter horizon. The night, therefore, appeared to be preordained. It was the symbol of inevitable doom, of the ongoing passages between life and death, as well as between death and the promise of redemption and ensuing eternal life. Night, in the medieval conception, appeared as a tragic but inevitable suspension of light and life between one's point of origin in the lowly world (birth) and one's heavenly point of destination (eternal life, symbolized by the absence of night and perennial light). Needless to say, this particular conception of night has very little in common with the concerns evoked by the work in this exhibition.

It was not until the beginning of the modern era, and, more specifically, the Enlightenment, that the night became reinvestigated

"NIGHT HATH A THOUSAND EYES."

JOHN LYLY[1]

POL, JEAN, AND HERMAN DE LIMBOURG

The Death of Christ from *The Belles Heures of Jean de France, Duc de Berry*, 1406–08/1409

Ink, tempera, and gold leaf on vellum

9 ³/₈ x 6 ⁵/₈ in.

The Metropolitan Museum of Art, The Cloisters Collection, 1954 (54.1.1)

from totally new perspectives and with notably different expectations. At that point, an unprecedented plethora of investigations of the nocturnal phenomenon – through scientific, philosophic, poetic, and artistic means – began to take place. These layers of interpretations of the night form the ideological bedrock of what we might call the modern conception of night, and, to a large degree, they continue to resonate in part with today's complex, rich visions of the night.

For instance, consider the following two quotes from the two titans of the Enlightenment, Hegel and Kant, which tell us so much about the way the nocturnal phenomenon arouses utterly divergent associations within us. According to Hegel:

> The sky is night, it is black. As air our atmosphere is transparent, and if it were completely pure we should only see the black sky. It is filled with vapors, however, and is, therefore, a disturbing medium.[3]

Kant, on the other hand, sees something quite different. In the famous conclusion of his *Critique of Practical Reason*, Kant explains:

> There are two things which imbue the mind with a feeling of admiration and reverence, ever renewed, and ever on the increase, the more frequently and the more perseveringly our thoughts are occupied with them: *the star-clad sky* there *above us*, and *the moral law within ourselves*.[4]

To Hegel, the master in the tradition of Western rationalism and the champion of absolute idealism, night is seen as a kind of disturbance; everything should have a cause, and everything should be comprehensible by reason – as the famous Hegelian statement goes, everything that is real is rational, and everything that is rational is real. Yet when it comes to the night, things don't seem so clear. Night comes as some kind of disturbance on the seamless course of pure rationality.

For Kant, this is not a problem: The fact that the nocturnal phenomenon is out of reach – incomprehensible, stretching out toward infinity – is precisely what he finds exciting. In fact, he sees this as a positive – as a sign that we can, though in ways difficult to conceive, be in touch with the infinite. Kant explains the level of fascination that the star-clad sky arouses in us – in terms that echo beautifully with the works presently on view by Vija Celmins, Thomas Ruff, Pat Steir, Vic Muniz, Marc Swanson, Robert Longo, Russell Crotty, Lauren Orchowski, Jennifer Coates, and Jen DeNike. To all these artists' postures in front of the spectacle of the star-clad sky, this excerpt from Kant applies wonderfully:

> There is no need that we should search after [the stars], or merely surmise them, as hidden in obscurities, or as having to be placed in a transcendent region beyond our horizon. We see them before us and connect them directly with the consciousness we have of our existence. The starting-point of [this experience] is the place which we occupy in the external world of the senses, and as for the connection in which we find ourselves placed, its dimension is widened to an immeasurable extent, with worlds upon worlds, systems upon systems, and moreover, limitless times, in respect of their periodic motions, their beginning and their continuance.[5]

For Hegel – whose major task in the development of Western thought was to introduce history as a central engine propelling all cultural forms (from religion to art) through sequences of moments that make sense together – night defines itself as a recurrent lack of sense. Night is primordially the absence of light, and, as such, it is conceived as a deficiency. In Hegel's words:

> Light has to encounter its *limit*. . . . Difference is external to it as the absence of light. . . . It is because of this abstraction that light now finds a limit or deficiency; and it is through this limit that it first manifests itself. . . . In order that something may be manifest, there must be something which is different from light. . . . Light as such is invisible, and in that nothing may be seen in it, pure light resembles pure *darkness*, it is obscure and tenebrous. If we see in pure light, then we are pure vision, but we do not as yet see anything. . . . Light only manifests itself as such after it has differentiated itself as light by distinguishing itself from shade.[6]

This powerful intuition presaged Cézanne's obsessive struggling, a century or so later, with the idea of representing pure light – the sun itself. This obsession finds its negative echo in a number of the works presented in this exhibition. For example, Hegel understood that, paradoxically, light is only visible through its absence, and one can very well read Laurent Grasso's evocative neon installation *Infinite Light* as an incarnation of Hegel's dialectic "Day for light for day for light for. . . ." For, as Hegel put it, light in itself, in its absolute purity, is invisible:

> There is an external relation between light and darkness, and the existence of light occurs on the boundary between them, in the being-for-other of which something is illuminated.[7]

This endless dialectical relationship is the very subject, of course, of Grasso's installation (which, almost literally, never ends) and it is also cogently explored in the works of artists such as Orchowski, David Claerbout, and others who utilize light in order to suggest darkness, and vice versa.

LAUREN ORCHOWSKI
Little Rocket, Starry Night (detail), 2007
Wood, metal, polymer, photographic paper, and fluorescent bulb
24 ¼ x 30 x 23 in.
Courtesy of the artist

The strength of Hegel's conception is that it established a necessary, mutually constitutive interconnection between day and night:

> Dark matter is primarily the negation of light, and constitutes
> the opposition to its abstractly identical ideality; it is opposition
> in its own self. It has material reality, and within itself falls apart
> into a *duality*.[8]

This interconnection is made tangible through numerous works in the present exhibition, from Coates's atmospheric paintings to Crotty's globes featuring renderings of stars and planets.

Whereas Hegel explores the conceptual negativity embodied in the tension and the cyclical complementary opposition between day and night, Kant – Hegel's nemesis – sees in night the gate to infinity. In this, one might initially believe that he is not far from a religious conception of the cosmos as a sign of the glory of God:

> The heavens declare the glory of God; and the firmament
> sheweth his handiwork. Day unto day uttereth speech, and night
> unto night sheweth knowledge.[9]

Except, of course, that Kant turns this order of priorities around; for him, the firmament puts us in touch not so much with God but with ourselves, insofar as we carry the feeling of God, or infinity, within ourselves. In other words, the firmament reflects the dimension of infinity that we carry within our small finite selves. The starry night exposes us to ourselves – no longer to God. Hence, we can now also better understand how "the star-clad sky above us" and the "moral law within ourselves" exist in parallel, mirroring each other: They both conjure up a dimension of infinity within *and* outside us.

It is here that we touch upon the other dimension within this exhibition, the dimension Kant alludes to: the fact that this "moral law within ourselves" that inspires "admiration and reverence" in the same way that gazing at the stars does is founded and dependent upon freedom. Indeed, there is no moral law within ourselves if it is forced upon us. The night is the space that opens up the gates of this awesome and frightening moral law within ourselves: The night, as we all know, is the moment when all things, all actions, become possible; the moment when we are in touch with our raw freedom. Numerous works in the *In the Heat of the Night* section of this exhibition explore precisely this aspect of the night, including those of Kohei Yoshiyuki, Shizuka Yokomizo, Deborah Stratman, Charles LaBelle, Marc Swanson and Neil Gust, and others. The moral law is, therefore, totally dependent on raw freedom – and this freedom is, in theory, infinite. Nothing can limit it – other than the freedom of others, which itself is, likewise, infinite.

Here Kant introduces a concept that is absolutely paramount to our modern, or even postmodern, conscience: The night not only mirrors this inner sense of infinity but also appears as a catalyst, as a liberating medium that propels pent-up drives, or pulsions ("Trieb") in the psychoanalytical sense. This exhibition abounds in examples illustrating the multitudinous (indeed, apparently infinite) possibilities here – from voyeurism to exhibitionism to the endless peripatetic cruising through bars and clubs of all kinds.

In her extraordinary book *Men in Dark Times*, Hannah Arendt makes a comment that seems to explain Kant's intuition in today's terms (and could well serve as the epigraph to this exhibition): "Whatever cannot become the object of discourse – the truly sublime, the truly horrible, or the uncanny – may find a human voice through which to sound into the world, but it is not exactly human."[10]

In the end, the main distinction between the modern foundation of the conception of night and today's visions (as articulated in "to: Night") is what Arendt cogently refers to as our capacity (or lack thereof) to "resist the weird irreality of this worldlessness." Gregory Crewdson certainly gives us a way to anchor this experience of the "weird irreality of the worldlessness" around us in concrete and tangible terms. For, as Katy Siegel beautifully argues in her text, we may well have lost, after all, the meaning of the night (if we ever mastered it). Siegel refers to an ongoing erosion of the night, where night and day seem to fuse into each other, into a gray, indistinguishable mass (again, Grasso's haunting metaphor comes to mind). For Arendt, "dark times" have replaced the night. She explains:

> The historical time, the "dark times" mentioned in the title, is,
> I think, visible everywhere. . . . I borrow the term from Brecht's
> famous poem "To Posterity," which mentions the disorder and
> the hunger, the massacres and the slaughterers, the outrage over
> injustice and the despair "when there was only wrong and no
> outrage" [Brecht], the legitimate hatred that makes you ugly
> nevertheless, the well-founded wrath that makes the voice grow
> hoarse.[11]

The dialectic between light and darkness takes on a completely different dimension when analyzed by Arendt in the context of our contemporary times: These dark times (the extent of which could only escape early modern thinkers such as Hegel and even Marx) within which we live are offset only by the faint, fake lighting produced by the establishment:

> When we think of dark times and of people living and moving
> in them, we have to take this camouflage, emanating from
> and spread by the "establishment" . . . into account. If it is the

function of the public realm to throw light on the affairs of
men by providing a space of appearances in which they can
show in deed and word, for better and worse, who they are and
what they can do, then darkness has come when this light is
extinguished by "credibility gaps" and "invisible government,"
by speech that does not disclose what is but sweeps it under the
carpet, by exhortations, moral and otherwise, that, under the
pretext of upholding old truths, degrade all truth to meaningless
triviality.[12]

This text, written in 1968, could have been written yesterday –
the pungency of Arendt's argument remains as sharp and alive as
ever. Nonetheless, it is from within the heart of darkness that we
may (and probably should) expect some illumination. This faint
note of optimism is also expressed in Arendt's voice:

Such illumination may well come less from theories and
concepts than from the uncertain, flickering, and often weak
light that some men and women, in their lives and their works,
will kindle under almost all circumstances. . . . Eyes so used to
darkness as ours will hardly be able to tell whether their light
was the light of a candle or that of a blazing sun.[13]

From Halina Kliem to Spencer Finch, this exhibition offers layers
of metaphorical and poetic responses to Hannah Arendt's simple,
powerful, and faintly hopeful voice – that, at the end of darkness,
comes the light.

—JOACHIM PISSARRO
BERSHAD PROFESSOR OF ART HISTORY &
DIRECTOR OF THE HUNTER COLLEGE ART
GALLERIES

1 John Lyly, *The Maid's Metamorphosis* (London, 1600).
2 See Margaret B. Freeman, "A Book of Hours Made for the Duke of Berry,"
   The Metropolitan Museum of Art Bulletin 15, no. 4 (December 1956): 93–104.
3 G. W. F. Hegel, *Philosophy of Nature*, vol. 2 (New York: Humanities Press, 1970), 149.
4 Immanuel Kant, *Critique of Practical Reason*, trans. H. W. Cassirer (Milwaukee, WI:
   Marquette University Press, 1998), 201. (Kant's italics.)
5 Ibid.
6 Hegel, *Philosophy of Nature*, 14. (Hegel's italics.)
7 Ibid., 22.
8 Ibid., 25. (Hegel's italics.)
9 Ps. 19:1, 2.
10 Hannah Arendt, *Men in Dark Times* (New York: Harcourt, Brace & World, Inc.,
   1968), 25.
11 Ibid., viii.
12 Ibid.
13 Ibid., ix–x.

GOOD NIGHT

Like other natural resources, night is disappearing. The ever-increasing concentration of human beings in cities and the electric glow that illuminates our presence (and even our absence) mean that most people never experience a true night sky, the enveloping disorientation of a darkness marked only by stars.

This change in the physical nature of night began with the nineteenth-century advent of gas and electric light. Paradoxically, the very processes of urbanization and industrialization that began to erode night led to a new valuation of it. Night's layered social meanings revolved around subjects, events, and experiences that existed before, outside, underneath, or in opposition to civilization. First among these, of course, was nature – the starry night – which, despite the new lights, reasserted itself when cities and people slept. Then human nature: love, sex, wild carousing, freedom, dreams. And nightmares, too; not all nocturnal activities were positive. Much of night's attraction lay in escape from social controls, its promise of the unconventional pleasures prized by bohemians, aristocrats, outcasts, poets, and, of course, artists. In the less extreme sense, night was the time for eating dinner, seeing one's family, meeting friends for a drink. Most fundamentally, night was, for most, the time not spent at work, under the control of those who bought labor time for money.

That was the Romantic night, and it lingers today. If there is a dominant motif, however, in the social criticism of the past thirty years, or at least that criticism prized by artists, it is the idea that capitalism has steadily encroached on our time, forcing people to work more – longer hours, multiple jobs, night shifts – and colonizing what was previously free time by converting it to "leisure," which centers around activities structured by purchases of goods and services or (as in TV-watching) permeated by advertising. From Raymond Williams to Guy Debord to Antonio Negri, writers have described an erosion of the strict boundary of work time – the limit set to capitalism's dominion over the self – as consumption became an activity that could fill all our waking hours. The glowing televisions featured in the classic mid-century photography of Robert Frank, Lee Friedlander, and others speak not only of alienation but also of this version of leisure time, distinguished from earlier forms of entertainment by reinforcing ties to the dominant social system rather than temporarily loosening them. Today, with the computer equally used for work and pleasure, many claim that leisure and even sleep ("dreaming in code") too closely resemble work and have been rendered productive.

Contemporary art institutions have eagerly participated in these changes. The "Long Night of Museums," which began in Germany in 1997 and spread through northern Europe, brings together museums and other cultural institutions to stay open late into the night. For "Nuit Blanche" ("white night" or "all-nighter"), first celebrated in Paris and now found from Tel Aviv to Lima, thousands of tourists flood cities after dark to see spectacular art events. Artists participate, lighting up the night or making a false night seemingly devoid of nature. Instead, there is culture, the artifice of the countless constructed versions of midnight suns and dramatically lit artworks, keeping to the sunny side of shopping, milling about, hitting the trail of art. Out at one of these events, it feels as if we are heading for the day when there is no night.

As nightlife becomes more official, more promoted as part of a liberal economic plan, less and less pictorial art celebrates the transgressive bacchanals of clubs and bars and parties so prevalent from Toulouse-Lautrec to Nan Goldin. (Night's disappearance is more sinister in the photographs and videos that mimic night surveillance images.) But forms of the Romantic night persist. Night skies abound, although the indifference to our presence that once seemed sublime now takes on a more pointedly apocalyptic air. The city walker also continues to wander, eyes fixed on the street instead of the sky, alert to the overlooked miracle of a sidewalk crack or involuntary tinfoil sculpture. While the poetry of the urban everyday persists, photographs show the suburban night more often dilapidated or otherwise pathetic, lacking historical patina and barely dignified by melancholy. The many abstract paintings evoking night imply a more beautiful solitude, the escape to the night studio, a remaining place of quiet in a crowded world. In a densely packed city, the artist's nighttime rhythms seem less an effort to defy social norms – to escape the 9-to-5 routine – than a way simply to avoid people. It's striking that nocturnal art is largely empty of human beings in a contemporary society that so values connectedness, interaction, mass leisure, and audience participation.

Night lingers most strongly perhaps as a metaphor, waxing full as literal night wanes. Recent exhibitions and artworks have featured night as a symbol for dimming, decay, even apocalypse (occasionally revealing an odd tone-deafness to the sound of "darkness" as a pejorative). Rendering the diurnal cycle on a historical scale, curators and artists, like social critics, have declared a new Dark Age, wherein current conditions evoke a return to the irrational, placing us at the end of a period, or even the world. At least in the United States, there is a general perception that the brilliant Enlightenment culture is dimming, or even that it never really took deep root here. Perhaps the post-war decades of affluence and progress barely covered a deep superstition and brutality that has resurfaced, echoing throughout the world the U.S. helped to shape. A kind of Romanticism without the romance dominates.

This sense of darkness, of collapse, is not always (only) metaphoric: While I was working on this essay, my New York neighborhood lost electrical power for twenty-four hours, the nineteenth-century power grid overtaxed by contemporary density and demands. How easily, how quickly, how early night – real night – fell. And how precarious our artificial daylight seemed.

– KATY SIEGEL
ASSOCIATE PROFESSOR OF ART HISTORY,
HUNTER COLLEGE

LAURENT GRASSO
Infinite Light, 2006/2008
Neon
Dimensions variable
Courtesy of the artist and Galerie Chez Valentin, Paris

One can't help but reflect upon the aptness of bringing Laurent Grasso's *Infinite Light* to Hunter College. As an institution of higher learning, Hunter specializes in bringing the light of wisdom to its students. And as an extension of the Art Department at Hunter College, the Hunter College Art Galleries attempt to extend that illumination into the public realm. Here, we specialize in knowledge, but also in creating connections between disciplines and presenting exhibitions for the benefit of students, faculty, artists, and the community. Grasso's work expands upon our mission. As part of the exhibition "to: Night" concurrently on view at the Bertha and Karl Leubsdorf Art Gallery and the Times Square Gallery, the work *Infinite Light* takes the show's theme outside the confines of the gallery walls and brings its message to the streets. Composed of the words "day for night" illuminated in neon and repeated in a continuous progression, the work spans the pedestrian bridges that link the Hunter buildings and acts as a metaphorical connection between the school and the art that is produced and exhibited here. Never in the history of the school has a project of this scale graced the exterior of its buildings, and realizing this project required support from many different areas of Hunter, the community, the city, and the art world. *Infinite Light's* bold and unique presentation acts as a kind of beacon or public announcement inviting those who see it into the galleries. In this way, the effect is very much in keeping with the traditional application of neon for commercial signage used to attract potential visitors.

In filmmaking parlance, the phrase "day for night" describes the now outdated illusory process of shooting during the day while using filters or a low lens aperture to produce the effect of night. In French, the technique is called *nuit Américaine* ("American night"), referring to this uniquely American innovation as well as its liberal use in American Westerns, B-movies, and *film noir*. A well-known film by François Truffaut from 1973 titled *La Nuit Américaine* stars the director and Jacqueline Bisset in a self-referential exploration of filmmaking and its real-life consequences. In his work, Truffaut focuses on the slippage between artifice and reality. Similarly, in *Infinite Light*, Grasso attempts to "construct ambiguity in a world where everything is clear and oriented" by choosing a concept that entails falsifying the most basic truth – night and day.

In Grasso's work, the blue filters used in the day-for-night technique serve as inspiration for the color of the neon letters themselves. As night falls, the glowing blue letters become pronounced against the darkness. The repetition of the words "day for night for day for night for day for night for" produces the effect of a continuous loop in which "day for night" is interchangeable with "night for day," thus conferring the effects of one upon the other. By concluding the piece on the word *for*, the artist implies the never-ending, inevitable process of day moving into night and becoming day again. This cycle is one of life's few absolutes.

As an artist, Grasso often places nature or reality in contrast with the false or artificial. In *Infinite Light*, he comments on time's natural progression while drawing attention to the lengths devised to subvert the natural order. Here, Grasso refers to the deceit involved in the cinematic practice of shooting day for night. By referencing this outdated, unconvincing technique, Grasso reminds us that the innate progression of time trumps the human effort to challenge it.

Working primarily in video, Grasso is keenly aware of the effects of light, which he uses here to achieve a distinctive result. There is a cinematic quality to the continuous chain of words as it creates a kind of panorama above the street. However, unlike film, *Infinite Light* makes no effort to present a straightforward narrative, but rather indicates the cyclical quality of our daily lives. Its striking presence creates a strong response even before its concept is fully grasped. In the artist's words, "people do not totally understand the work at first but at the same time are seduced by what they see." The work offers an open invitation for consideration of its deeper meaning.

Infinite Light transforms the landscape of the city. The neon words crossing Lexington Avenue and 68th Street draw attention to the temporal nature of the skyline as the silhouette of its architecture emerges and recedes throughout the day's cycle. The horizontality of the work acts as a kind of simulated horizon line that moves from east to west, marking the course of the sun in its daily trajectory. Grasso uses this artificial apparatus to focus our attention on the natural phenomenon of time, reminding us that although we often focus on the long term, it is the daily passage of time that cumulatively makes up a lifetime.

– TRACY L. ADLER
   CURATOR, HUNTER COLLEGE ART GALLERIES

STARRY NIGHTS

VIJA CELMINS
JENNIFER COATES
RUSSELL CROTTY
JEN DeNIKE
HALINA KLIEM
ROBERT LONGO
VIK MUNIZ
LAUREN ORCHOWSKI
THOMAS RUFF
PAT STEIR
MARC SWANSON

"THE STARRY HEAVEN,
THOUGH IT OCCURS SO VERY
FREQUENTLY TO OUR VIEW,
NEVER FAILS TO EXCITE AN
IDEA OF GRANDEUR."
EDMUND BURKE[1]

Surely no natural spectacle is more universal than a star-filled sky. Glimmering celestial bodies have awed and inspired humanity for centuries, and despite significant scientific and technological advancements, they continue to be a favorite subject for many contemporary artists. The works in the *Starry Nights* section of this exhibition include numerous representations of stars and galaxies in an array of media. For many of the artists represented here, their fascination stems from the great distances starlight must travel to reach Earth. Some cite their love of astronomy and incorporate scientific instruments and data to into their artistic processes. Others use the composition and reduced palette of white dots on a black field as an exercise in abstract composition. In all cases, their representations of the night sky reveal, as the epigraph suggests, that although there is perhaps nothing more commonplace than day fading into night, the stars remain a fertile – and sometimes surprising – subject for artistic examination.

Thomas Ruff's "Stern" series (plate IX) comprises highly detailed, large-scale C-prints made from negatives Ruff purchased from the European Southern Observatory. By opting for a large format and specifying the dimensions and orientation, Ruff essentially creates an abstract black-and-white composition that is also a scientific record of the stars. Vija Celmins also refers to photographic source material when creating her starscapes, which simultaneously represent deep space and a flat surface through a pattern of white dots against a black background. *Strata* (plate I), a mezzotint print, is a portrait of cosmic infinity (Celmins locates stars that are thousands of light years away) but the image can also be appreciated as a two-dimensional abstraction. Robert Longo's *Horse Head Nebula* (plate VI) is a meticulous charcoal drawing of a cloud of indistinguishable glowing gaseous material light years away. Like Ruff and Celmins, Longo also relates the natural phenomenon of starry nights to abstract art, applying photorealist drawing technique to a nonfigurative subject with a monochromatic palette. Pat Steir's *Starry Night* (plate X) is a photogravure and aquatint whose freeform explosion of stars recalls the fluidity and motion of Jackson Pollock's drips. However, Steir maintains that abstraction and representation are one and the same in her depictions of the night sky. Russell Crotty, himself an amateur astronomer, uses a powerful telescope to observe and record the details of stars and planets. *Venus Over High Glade* (plate III) – a scrupulous rendering of the night sky transferred in ink and watercolor onto a three-dimensional spherical structure – inverts our usual view of the night sky. Crotty's globe-drawing creates a way for us to view celestial bodies from an impossible external vantage point. In his "Pictures of Air" series, Vik Muniz also challenges our perception of stars and planets. By photographing gelatin infused with air, Muniz creates a black-and-white image that looks convincingly like a series of galaxies. Based on a computerized rendering of

the sky as Columbus would have seen it on October 11, 1492, *Viewing from Guanahani, Bahamas* (plate VII) is perhaps ideally observed in context of this exhibition. When displayed alongside photographs of the actual stars, such as Ruff's *Stern 17h 51m/-22°*, Muniz's night-sky illusion is truly put to the test. The stars in Marc Swanson's *Boy in Tree* (plate XI) have personal, rather than scientific, resonance. The silhouette of a young boy in the upper branches of a tree is a nostalgic reference to childhood wonderment of the night sky, and the glitter used to represent the stars is a nod to the sparkle and dazzle of the gay nightclub and disco scene. Jen DeNike's photo installation *What Do You Believe In* (plate IV) comprises eighteen 8-by-10-inch photographs that are collaged with found imagery of stars originally captured by NASA's Hubble Space Telescope. Standing in front of the composite starry background, a female figure is shown using naval semaphore flag language to spell out the title of this work. Halina Kliem's *I Want To See Stars* (plate V) is a DVD loop in which a hand repeats the simple gesture of switching a light bulb on and off. An extended viewing of the flashing evokes twinkling stars. Lauren Orchowski's "diorama theaters" are presented in a dark room in which the only visible light appears through pinpricks on photographic paper used to represent a star-filled sky. In *Little Rocket, Starry Night* (plate VIII), Orchowski creates an idealized environment devoid of artificial light and filled with swirls of stars that recall the brush strokes in van Gogh's *Starry Night* (1889). Jennifer Coates also finds inspiration in van Gogh's nocturnal landscapes. In her painting *Blackblood and Twinkle* (plate II), Coates builds upon the Dutch master's ability to represent the brilliance of stars and creates mesmerizing hyperbolic twinkles in the night sky.

— MARA HOBERMAN
CURATOR

1 Edmund Burke, *A Philosophical Enquiry into the Origin of Our Idea of the Sublime and Beautiful* (1757).

I VIJA CELMINS
Strata, 1982
One-color mezzotint, from 25 individual copperplates mounted on a single aluminum plate
29 ½ x 35 ½ in.
Courtesy of McKee Gallery, New York

II   JENNIFER COATES
Blackblood and Twinkle, 2004
Acrylic on canvas
72 x 60 in.
Courtesy of Kinz, Tillou + Feigen, New York

III   RUSSELL CROTTY

Venus Over High Glade, 2006

Ink and watercolor on paper on fiberglass sphere

12 x 12 x 12 in.

Courtesy of the artist and Hosfelt Gallery, New York and San Francisco

IV   JEN DeNIKE

What Do You Believe In, 2008
Eighteen black-and-white photographs
8 x 10 in. each
Courtesy of Smith-Stewart, New York

V   HALINA KLIEM

I Want To See Stars, 2004

Single-channel digital video installation

2 minutes

Courtesy of DUVE Berlin

VII   VIK MUNIZ

Viewing from Guanahani, Bahamas from "Pictures of Air," 2001

C-print

60 x 48 in.

Courtesy of the artist and Sikkema Jenkins & Co., New York

VIII   LAUREN ORCHOWSKI

Little Rocket, Starry Night, 2007

Wood, metal, polymer, photographic paper, and fluorescent bulb

24 ¼ x 30 x 23 in.

Courtesy of the artist

IX   THOMAS RUFF
Stern 17h 51m/-22°, 1990
C-print
102 ⅝ x 74 in.
Private collection, New Jersey

X   PAT STEIR

Starry Night, 2000

Photogravure, aquatint, and pochoir

28 $^7/_8$ x 25 $^3/_8$ in.

Courtesy of Pace Prints, New York

XI MARC SWANSON
Boy in Tree, 2005
Glass, enamel, and glitter
36 x 24 in.
Private collection, New Jersey

CITY NIGHTS ... ○○

STAN DOUGLAS
EWAN GIBBS
DAVID HAMMONS
YVONNE JACQUETTE
BARNEY KULOK
BRITTA LUMER
VERA LUTTER
FLORIAN MAIER-AICHEN
JOHN PILSON

COUNTRY NIGHTS ... ○○

DAVID CLAERBOUT
TIM DAVIS
JULIANE EIRICH
TODD HIDO
DOINA KRAAL

Nightfall affects the landscape in a variety of interesting ways, often accentuating topographical features in a manner that wholly transforms a particular environment. At night, the natural landscape tends to fade into darkness while man-made structures illuminated by artificial-light sources emerge from their surroundings – seeming almost to come alive as night falls. As Maugham's quote suggests, the suburban and bucolic nocturnal landscapes are generally depicted as tranquil (at times hauntingly so), whereas the city by night appears energized and, in many cases, frenetic. The works in the *City Nights...Country Nights...* section of this exhibition illustrate this dichotomy through numerous examples of urban versus suburban nocturnal scenes.

The urban scenes in this section are unified by their accent on vibrant color and activity. Although they share an overarching sense of high-voltage nightlife, these works are varied both in terms of medium and perspective. In *Phat Free* (plate XIV), David Hammons focuses on the action of a man who kicks a can while roaming New York City streets. The constant activity and sound remind us that night in the city is never totally dark, quiet, or still. Choosing a totally different approach and technique for *Untitled* (plate XIX), Florian Maier-Aichen positions his camera at a great distance from his subject in order to show the preternaturally bright lights of a metropolis penetrating through miles of night sky. This manipulated, composite image is less a portrait of a specific city than a stylized impression of urban light pollution interrupting the otherwise dark sky.

Ewan Gibbs uses pencil on paper to achieve high contrast pixilated renderings of familiar urban scenes. By stripping the skyline represented in *London* (plate XIII) of hyper-real photographic detail, Gibbs creates a moody and intriguing portrait of London by night. John Pilson's *Dark Empire* (plate XX) is a continuous 25-minute video depicting the New York City skyline during the evening of the 2003 blackout. By positioning the Empire State Building in the center of the frame, Pilson captures what is perhaps the most iconic skyline in the world as it disappears into complete blackness. *Dark Empire* is a striking, frightening vision that reminds us that the urban environment has come to be defined in direct opposition to night's natural darkness.

Yvonne Jacquette also focuses her attention on New York City in her painting *Above Times Square* (plate XV), in this case emphasizing the buildings' glowing presence against the night sky. Jacquette explores the variety of quality and color in the lights that make the city sparkle and shine at night. Stan Douglas's *Every Building on 100 West Hastings* (plate XII) is a panoramic photograph of one of Vancouver's most notorious blocks. Although the storefronts and apartment buildings lining the street appear derelict and uncared for, the dark sky, the glow of the street lamps, and the overall still-ness of the image lend a certain elegance to Douglas's ode to his native city's gritty Eastside.

Barney Kulok explores the abundant artificial light sources that pervade urban landscapes, including billboards, floodlights, and neon signage. The digital transparency lightbox *Skillman Avenue, Queens NY* (plate XVI) shows a glowing billboard advertisement whose light reflects uncanny colors onto the bleak chain-link fence and empty parking lot below. The lightbox format accentuates Kulok's observation that the color spectrum of a city night is not dark and subdued but rather full of electrifying shades ranging from hot pink to ultramarine blue. In contrast, Britta Lumer's ink drawings are washes of gray and black that create evocative cityscapes. *Nachtstadt/City at Night III* (plate XVII) does not repre-sent one city in particular but is an homage to the city by night as characterized by artificial light. Vera Lutter uses an enormous camera obscura to capture haunting "day-for-night" images of urban architecture. The finished photographs, such as *30th Street Station, Philadelphia, II: April 17, 2006* (plate XVIII), are negatives that situate glowing, ghostly urban landscapes against a menacing dark sky.

Even the most mundane suburban street becomes eerily enchant-ed when seen though Todd Hido's camera lens. Hido, who photographs predominantly lower-income suburban neighbor-hoods, works almost exclusively at night, using only available light. His photograph *1738* (plate XXIV) depicts a parked car illumi-nated through dense fog by a lone street lamp. The soft, hazy glow artfully suggests a supernatural force pervading an otherwise deso-late tableau. Tim Davis also forgoes flash when photographing suburban landscapes. In his "Illilluminations" series, Davis focuses on discrepancies created when artificial light is imposed upon the night environment. In *Bradford Pear* (plate XXII), Davis presents an incongruously spot-lit pear tree, whose blown-out presence appears ghost-like and dramatic in comparison to the deep muted tones of the surrounding parking lot. Juliane Eirich observes popular leisure destinations that are action-packed during the day but left vacant at night. Her panoramic photograph *Beach Chairs* (plate XXIII) depicts a dark beach lined with empty lounge chairs, revealing how commonplace man-made objects can become purely aesthetic once their functionality has been stripped away by the darkness and emptiness of night. Doina Kraal's installa-tion *Sprookjesbos 2* (plate XXV) is a fantasy environment suggesting a forest of moonlit trees. By projecting images of foliage onto hanging aluminum tree-shaped forms, Kraal creates an en-chanted forest both bewitching and beautiful – much like the dark woods described in fairytales. David Claerbout's photographs are presented here as transparencies in lightboxes – a format well suited to emphasizing glowing light sources. Claerbout, however, reclaims the florescent-lit medium as an appropriate display for night photography and, ironically, as a way to draw attention to darkness. Displayed in a room without any ambient light, the distinctly suburban landscape of highway lanes, grass, and trees in *Nightscape Lightbox (second)* (plate XXI) slowly becomes visible as the viewer's eyes adjust to the nearly complete darkness.

— MARA HOBERMAN
CURATOR

1 W. Somerset Maugham, *A Writer's Notebook* (London: William Heinemann, 1949).

XII   STAN DOUGLAS

Every Building on 100 West Hastings, 2001

C-print

23 ½ x 96 in.

Courtesy of David Zwirner, New York

XIII   EWAN GIBBS
       London, 2005
       Pencil on paper
       16 ½ x 23 ⅜ in.
       Collection of Glenn Fuhrman, New York
       Courtesy of The FLAG Art Foundation, New York

XIV   DAVID HAMMONS
Phat Free, 1995–1999
Videotape transferred to DVD, paper, and paperboard box
5:02 minutes
Courtesy of Zwirner & Wirth, New York

XVI   BARNEY KULOK
Skillman Avenue, Queens NY, 2004
Digital transparency in lightbox
20 x 24 in.
Courtesy of the artist and Nicole Klagsbrun Gallery

XVII   BRITTA LUMER
Nachtstadt/City at Night III, 2006
Indian ink on Ingres paper
19 ¾ x 25 ⅔ in.
Courtesy of the artist and Galerie Morgen, Berlin

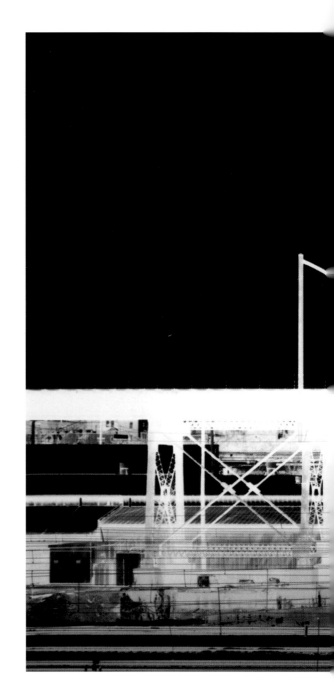

XVIII   VERA LUTTER

30th Street Station, Philadelphia, II: April 17, 2006, 2006

Silver gelatin print

31 ½ x 57 ½ in.

© Vera Lutter. Courtesy of Gagosian Gallery, New York

XIX   FLORIAN MAIER–AICHEN
      Untitled, 2005
      C-print
      69 ¾ x 92 ½ in.
      Collection of David and Kim Schrader

XXI   DAVID CLAERBOUT

Nightscape Lightbox (second), 2002–2003

Black anodized aluminum lightbox, Cibachrome mounted on Plexiglas with protection layer

49 ¼ x 57 ½ x 7 ⅞ in.

Courtesy of Rennie Collection, Vancouver, Canada

XXII   TIM DAVIS
Bradford Pear from "Illilluminations," 2004
C-print
48 x 60 in.
Courtesy of the artist and Greenberg Van Doren Gallery, New York

XXIII JULIANE EIRICH
Beach Chairs, 2004
C-print mounted on Alu-Dibond
36 x 96 in.
Courtesy of Peter Poby, New York

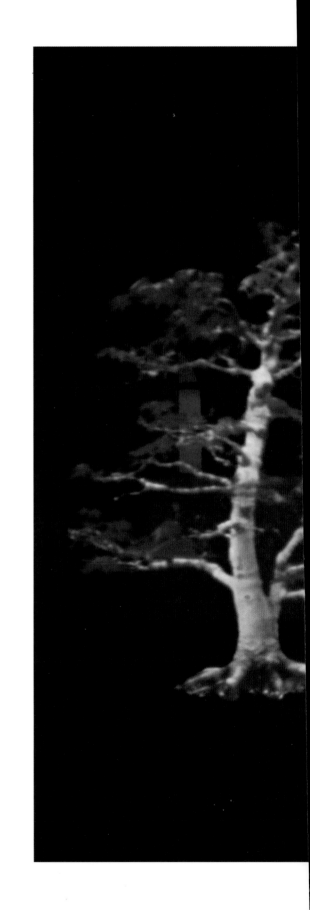

XXV   DOINA KRAAL

Sprookjesbos 2, 2005

Painted aluminum trees cut-outs with slide projection

Dimensions variable

Courtesy of the artist and Soledad Senlle Gallery, Amsterdam

IN THE HEAT OF THE NIGHT

GREGORY CREWDSON
NEIL GUST
CHARLES LaBELLE
THOMAS RUFF
DEBORAH STRATMAN
MARC SWANSON
SHIZUKA YOKOMIZO
KOHEI YOSHIYUKI

"MOST GLORIOUS NIGHT!
THOU WERT NOT SENT FOR SLUMBER!"
LORD BYRON[1]

Natural darkness is seductive. The same dark skies that designate a time for sleep also inspire deviancy – including predatory, exhibitionist, voyeuristic, and other questionable conduct. Titillating glimpses of nighttime activity are presented in this section of the exhibition. The works included here often subvert night's assumed role as a cloaking agent. The romantic notion of natural darkness providing cover for clandestine activity seems quaint and archaic given our round-the-clock lifestyle and highly monitored contemporary society. So much of what we do in the dark can be – and *is* – easily observed and recorded.

Kohei Yoshiyuki's "The Park" series (plate XXXII) reveals late-night trysts using the combined technology of flash and infrared film. The photographs capture couples and groups engaging in sex acts in a public park, as well as expose a sizable population of voyeurs who watch from behind trees and bushes. Deborah Stratman also appropriates surveillance technology, depicting an arrest/escape sequence on infrared film in her video *In Order Not To Be Here* (plate XXIX). Here, as in "The Park" series, the grainy and crude effect of the infrared technology exaggerates the morbid fascination with nighttime's more indecorous activities. It is simultaneously thrilling and shameful to bear witness to something we ought not to see and that is only visible with the assistance of technology. In his "Nacht" series, Thomas Ruff creates an ominous portrait of Dusseldorf, Germany, by using a night-vision enhancer. Ordinarily innocuous subject matter, such as the terraced apartment building in *Nacht 2 I* (plate XXVIII), takes on a sinister quality when mediated by equipment closely associated with military surveillance.

Finding true obscurity at night is increasingly challenging because of near-constant interruption by artificial light sources. Though night may not guarantee literal invisibility, the precious hours of natural darkness do provide a means for escape – at least symbolically. The video installation by Marc Swanson and Neil Gust, *Love is all Around* (plate XXX), focuses on the after-hours scene at a gay nightclub. Presented in a small room lined with black Plexiglas, the projected interspliced images of glittering curtains, a bare-chested man, and pulsating strobe lights are reflected on the mirror-like surface of the dark plastic. In this environment, the viewer/voyeur becomes totally immersed in, and by proxy complicit in, the eroticism of the subject. Charles LaBelle documents nighttime activities in his "Driftworks" series. In his collaged "compound photograph" *Driftworks-Barcelona (Gothic Quarters, Night)* (plate XVII), LaBelle creates a nocturnal portrait of Barcelona that provides evidence of a wide variety of after-dark escapades. The creative process for Shizuka Yokomizo's "Dear Stranger" series (plate XXXI) begins when the artist leaves an anonymous letter asking the recipient to stand alone at his or her apartment window at a specified evening hour, so that the artist can take a photo from the street. Because the photographer is in the dark and the participant bathed in light, it is impossible for the subject to view the photographer. This scenario creates a complicit voyeur/exhibitionist relationship between artist and subject. In contrast to the more reportage-style representation of after-hours activity included in this section, Gregory Crewdson's photographs feature staged, psychologically charged nighttime scenes that accentuate the disquietude associated with people being active at night instead of tucked safely away in their beds. In *Untitled (penitent girl)* (plate XXVI), from Crewdson's "Twilight" series, a young woman stands on a dark suburban sidewalk clad only in her underwear, bowing her head in shame as she is confronted by an older woman who has pulled her car up to the curb to unload groceries. This mysterious and disturbing scene suggests numerous possible, and likely indecent, narratives.

– MARA HOBERMAN
CURATOR

1 Lord Byron, *Childe Harold's Pilgrimage* (1812–1818).

XXVI GREGORY CREWDSON
Untitled (penitent girl), 2001–2002
Digital C-print
48 x 60 in.
Collection of Dr. Bernard and JoAnn Kruger, New York

XXVII   CHARLES LaBELLE

Driftworks – Barcelona (Gothic Quarters, Night), 2005

Compound photograph

27 x 33 in.

Courtesy of Anna Kustera Gallery, New York

XXIX DEBORAH STRATMAN
In Order Not To Be Here, 2002
Video transfer from 16mm film
33 minutes
Courtesy of the artist

XXX   MARC SWANSON & NEIL GUST
Love is all Around, 2007
Video
3:51 minutes
Courtesy of artists and Bellwether, New York

XXXI   SHIZUKA YOKOMIZO
Stranger (10), 1999
C-print
50 x 42 ½ in.
Courtesy of the artist

XXXII KOHEI YOSHIYUKI
Untitled, 1971
Gelatin silver print
20 x 24 in.
© Kohei Yoshiyuki
Courtesy of Yossi Milo Gallery, New York

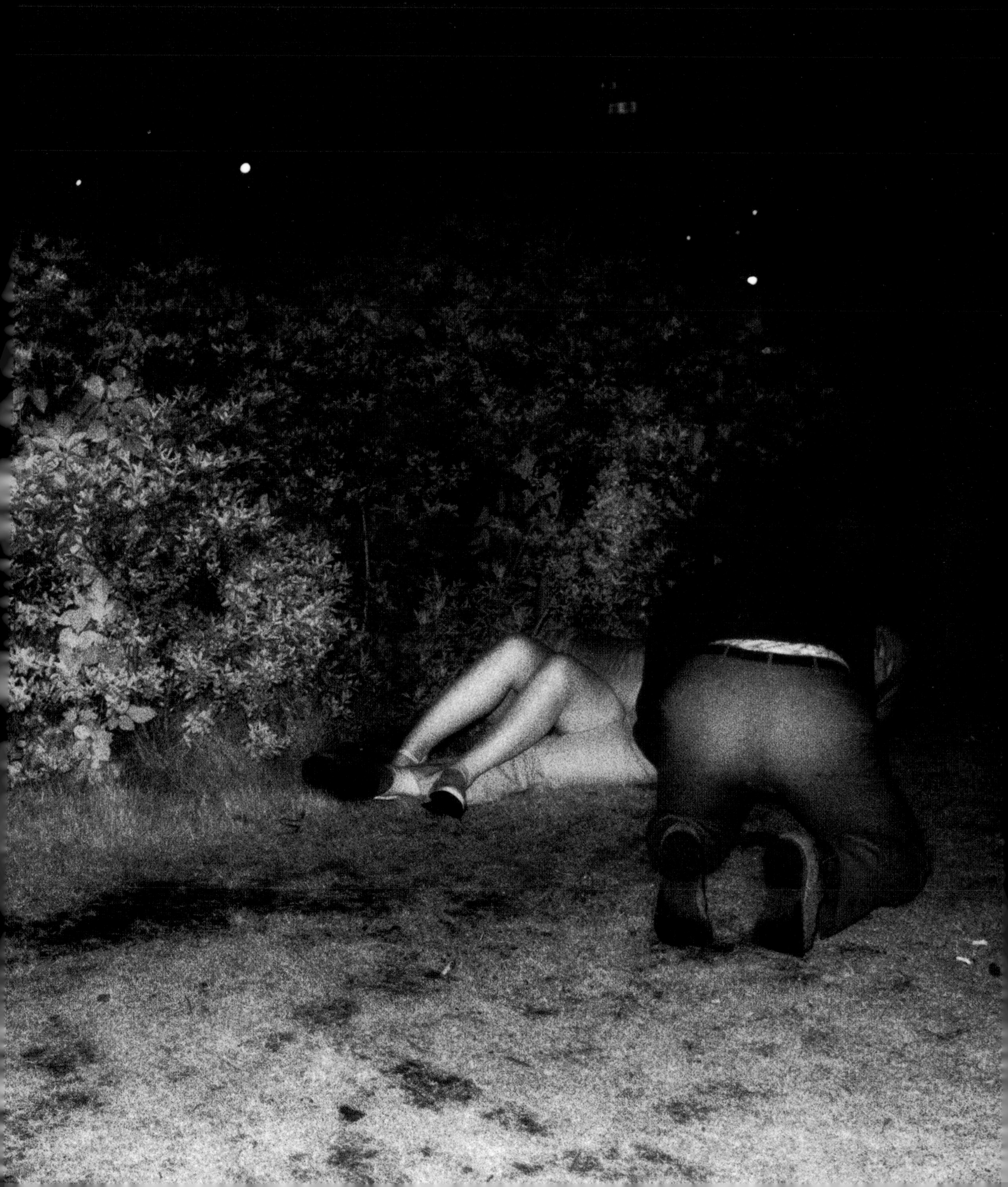

WHILE YOU WERE SLEEPING

SUSAN GRAHAM

YEON JIN KIM

CLAUDE LÉVÊQUE

JEFF WALL

ANDY WARHOL

"THE REPOSE OF SLEEP REFRESHES ONLY THE BODY. IT RARELY SETS THE SOUL AT REST. THE REPOSE OF THE NIGHT DOES NOT BELONG TO US. IT IS NOT THE POSSESSION OF OUR BEING. SLEEP OPENS WITHIN US AN INN FOR PHANTOMS. IN THE MORNING WE MUST SWEEP OUT THE SHADOWS."

GASTON BACHELARD[1]

Sleep is a phenomenon experienced by all, yet it remains an intriguing enigma. Numerous states of consciousness can be encompassed by the term. This section of the exhibition explores some of the many facets of sleep, such as deep sleep, dreams, nightmares, and insomnia.

Sleep (plate XXXVII) is Andy Warhol's first film, shot in 1963 with a 16mm camera. It depicts, quite literally, a man sleeping. The slumbering individual is John Giorno, a renowned poet and close friend of the artist. Although the film appears to depict the poet sleeping for a single continuous night (the film runs approximately six hours), Warhol actually recorded the footage in several sessions over a period of several months. Moreover, the film is constructed from repetitive footage, with sequences running several times over the six-hour timeframe. Through this deconstruction and reconstruction, Warhol creates an illusion of sleep, drawing attention to the distorted perception that often accompanies it. In *POPism* he gives a playful explanation for the motivation behind *Sleep*: "I could never finally figure out if more things happened in the sixties because there was more awake time for them to happen (since so many people were on amphetamines) or if people started taking amphetamines because there were so many things to do them in. . . . Seeing everybody so up all the time made me think that sleep was becoming pretty obsolete, so I decided I'd better quickly do a movie of a person sleeping." [2]

Sleep is not always serene and stress-free. Similarly, insomnia can be a disagreeable and disorienting experience, causing the mind to race and bounce between repetitive ideas and images. With *Insomnia* (plate XXXIII), an installation comprising hundreds of handmade, filigree egg-white-and-sugar beds installed in a repetitive circular formation, Susan Graham attempts to capture this no-man's land between sleep and consciousness, when one desperately desires sleep yet remains awake in a half-conscious mode. *Insomnia* is a poignant evocation of this ordeal.

Insomnia and despair seem to be the underlying themes of Jeff Wall's pigmented ink-jet print *After "Spring Snow" by Yukio Mishima, chapter 34* (plate XXXVI), one of the artist's most recent works in color that is not a lightbox. Set in Tokyo in 1912, this piece tells the story of Sakoto, the newlywed from Mishima's novel. Sakoto has suffered a sleepless night after an adulterous rendezvous on the beach with her lover. She is pictured in a Ford Model T, turning her back to the viewer to hide her face and her shame. Distraught, she pours sand from her shoe in an effort to conceal the evidence of her escapade from her maid, who might reveal her secret to her husband.

In her videos *Dreams . . .* (plate XXXIV), Yeon Jin Kim explores her dreams that are haunted by her fear of displacement from Korea to New York. To confront her dreams, Kim built a three-dimensional house-shaped model in which she incorporated a small camera that navigated the house. She used this model to deconstruct and reconstruct her dreams, subsequently building new narratives and fantasies from them.

French artist Claude Lévêque focuses on dreams, nightmares, and the subjective content of sleep. One of his most recent works is a neon installation that reads in French: *La nuit pendant que vous dormez je détruis le monde* ("At night while you are sleeping I destroy the world") (plate XXXV). Through this ominous statement (which also serves as the title of the work), the artist seems to cast himself as an angel of death, destroying the viewer's dreams and hopes while he or she is sleeping. Nighttime is portrayed as a time when the mind loses track of time and reality, and unrealistic hopes and secret fantasies may become real. Lévêque reminds us that sleep is a vulnerable state when one is left defenseless against various demons and supernatural forces.

—JULIA MORENO
CURATOR

1   Gaston Bachelard, *The Poetics of Reverie* (New York: The Orion Press, 1960).
2   Andy Warhol and Pat Hackett, *POPism* (New York: Harcourt, 1980).

XXXIV   YEON JIN KIM
Dreams . . . , 2008
Single-channel video
Courtesy of the artist

la nuit pendant que vous dormez, je détruis le monde

XXXVI   JEFF WALL
   After "Spring Snow" by Yukio Mishima, chapter 34, 2004
   C-print
   25 ½ x 29 in.
   Courtesy of Marian Goodman Gallery, New York

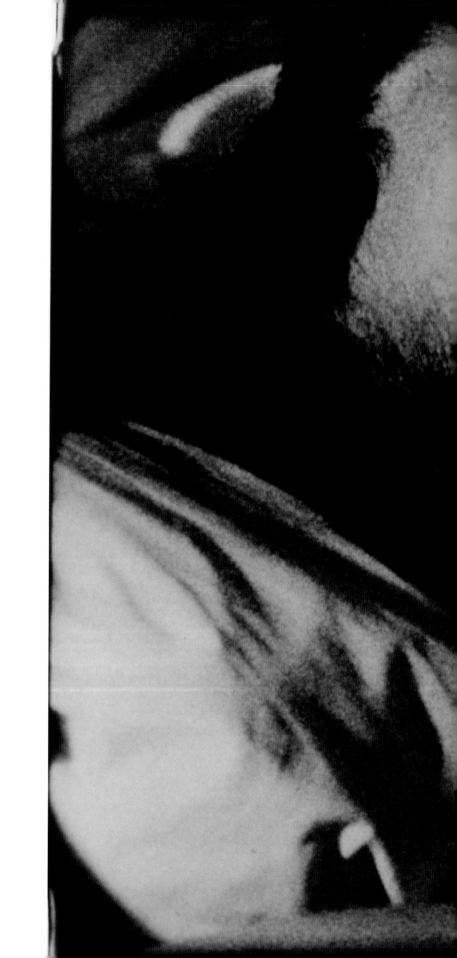

XXXVII ANDY WARHOL
Sleep, 1963
16mm black-and-white silent film
5 hours and 21 minutes
© 2008 The Andy Warhol Museum, Pittsburgh, Pa.,
a museum of Carnegie Institute

THE COLOR OF NIGHT

SEBASTIAN BEAR-McCLARD
SUSAN CRILE
SPENCER FINCH
LAURENT GRASSO
BARNEY KULOK
SUSANNA THORNTON
THOMAS WEAVER
JOHN ZURIER

"I OFTEN THINK THAT
THE NIGHT IS MORE
ALIVE AND MORE RICHLY
COLORED THAN THE DAY."
VINCENT VAN GOGH[1]

Whereas the glory of day has been much celebrated, nighttime is often associated with darkness and obscurity. Night's beauty pales in comparison to daytime's overt charms. Despite this – or perhaps because of it – many artists have been touched and inspired by the night, as van Gogh's quote reminds us. Some artists in this show work with the notion of night as darkness, or the absence of light. Others perceive night as a more positive force, a source of new colors and impressions to analyze and depict, either in an abstract mode or more naturalistically.

In his work, Spencer Finch explores the rich chromatic quality of night. To create the fluorescent-light sculpture *Moonlight (Luna County, New Mexico, July 13, 2003)* (plate XL), Finch observed the many colors that could be seen during a full moon in Luna County, New Mexico, on July 13th, 2003. Using a colorimeter, an optical device that measures the hue and saturation of color, Finch precisely measured the light of the full moon in order to artificially replicate it using a Color Resolution Index (CRI) fluorescent tube wrapped in strips of translucent blue and violet filters.

Using the real world as a starting point for an exploration of abstraction and the irrational, Susanna Thornton focuses on the abstract nature of light and color in her "NIGHTSTILLS" (plate XLII) series. Thornton's long-exposure nighttime photographs convey a sense of magic as the artist explores the fine line between abstraction and figuration.

In their video *River of Shadows* (plate XXXVIII), Sebastian Bear-McClard and Barney Kulok explore the effects of artificial light on objects at night. The actual light sources – neon signs, lightbox advertisements – remain out of the images' frames. These eerie scenes depict the transformation of ordinary neighborhood walls, rooftops, buildings, and car windows into mysterious urban abstractions.

Thomas Weaver's painting *Morning After Curtain* (plate XLIII) picks up on our difficulty distinguishing color at night and the effect this has on our sense of physical space. This painting suggests a brightly lit interior, indicated by a richly colored blue curtain. By using an interference-medium glaze to paint the curtain, Weaver achieves a subtle transparency effect between the inside and outside world, in which the color from the curtain seeps into the dark, muted tones of the night outside the window.

For his "Night" series (plate XLIV), John Zurier uses the uncommon medium of distemper, a combination of pigment and warm glue developed in medieval times and later employed by Vuillard and Matisse. Zurier applies several layers of paint on raw linen,

producing deep-blue monochromatic paintings. Vertical green lines that spread throughout the painting act as anchor points, accentuating the viewer's perception of depth. The result is an intense and vibrant visual experience in which the viewer feels immersed in the darkness of the painting.

At the end of the first Gulf War, hundreds of oil wells were detonated by the retreating Iraqis in the Burgan fields in Kuwait. Within a matter of seconds, the oil fields were engulfed in flames. In *Charred Earth* (plate XXXIX), Susan Crile depicts the infinite number of colors generated by the fire. In a striking contrast, the bright orange and red of the fire become inextricably linked to the darkness of the night.

In Laurent Grasso's video *L'éclipse* (plate XLI), the colors of the night reach their climax. This blended montage of a total solar eclipse and a sunset reveals rarely seen lights and colors. Night and day join forces to become one entity, transcending their traditional boundaries. By combining two natural phenomena and removing them from their original context, Grasso creates what he calls his own "false miracle."

—JULIA MORENO
CURATOR

1 Vincent van Gogh, *Complete Letters of Vincent Van Gogh* (Boston: Bulfinch, 2000).

XXXVIII   SEBASTIAN BEAR–McCLARD
          & BARNEY KULOK
          River of Shadows: SURFACE TENSION (N40° 44.499, W–73° 56.791), 2005
          Digital video loop
          19:32 minutes
          Courtesy of the artists and Nicole Klagsbrun Gallery, New York

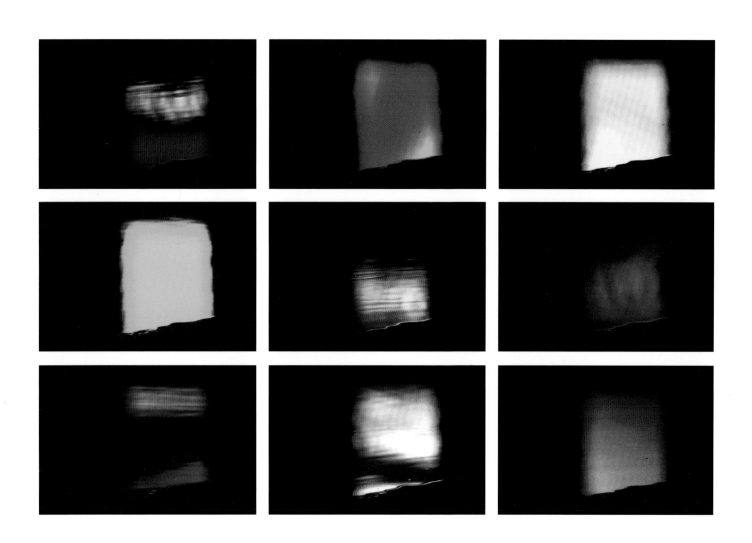

XXXIX   SUSAN CRILE
Charred Earth, 1994
Pumice, charcoal, oil stick, and pastel on paper
38 x 50 in.
Courtesy of the artist

XL   SPENCER FINCH
Moonlight (Luna County, New Mexico, July 13, 2003), 2003
Fluorescent bulb, and fixture filters
36 x 2 ½ in.
Courtesy of the artist

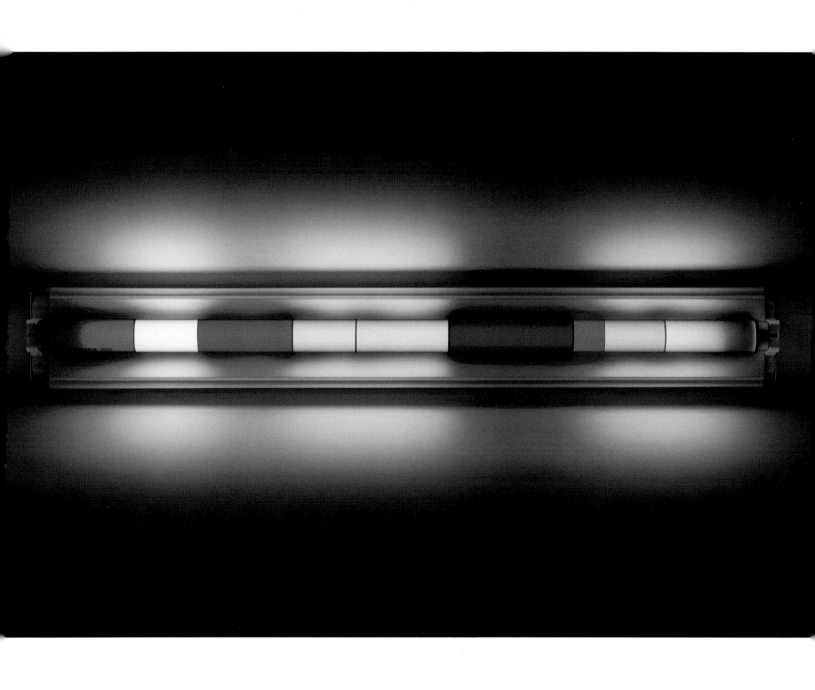

XLI   LAURENT GRASSO

L'éclipse, 2006

DVD projection

Courtesy of Galerie Chez Valentin, Paris

XLII SUSANNA THORTON
Rainbow/Shadow from "NIGHTSTILLS," 2004
Color photographic C-print mounted on Plexiglas
40 x 50 in.
Courtesy of the artist

XLIII   THOMAS WEAVER
         Morning After Curtain, 2008
         Acrylic on paper
         48 x 60 in.
         Courtesy of the artist

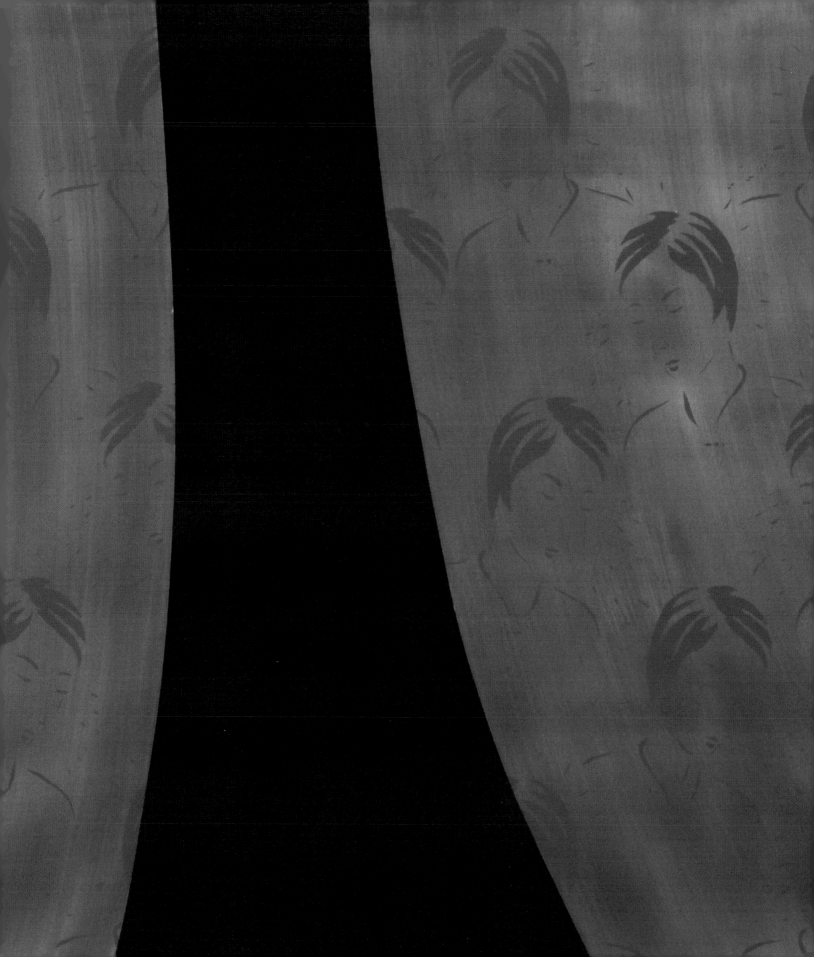

XLIV JOHN ZURIER
Night 16, 2007
Distemper on linen
30 x 20 in.
Courtesy of the artist

CHECKLIST OF THE EXHIBITION

Sebastian Bear-McClard and Barney Kulok
River of Shadows: BIG WINDOW
(N 40° 44.378, W-73° 56.749), 2005
Digital video loop; 20:30 minutes
Courtesy of the artists and Nicole Klagsbrun Gallery, New York

Sebastian Bear-McClard and Barney Kulok
River of Shadows: STEAM
(N 40° 44.391, W-73° 56.827), 2005
Digital video loop; 21:59 minutes
Courtesy of the artists and Nicole Klagsbrun Gallery, New York

Sebastian Bear-McClard and Barney Kulok
River of Shadows: SURFACE TENSION
(N 40° 44.499, W-73° 56.791), 2005
Digital video loop; 19:32 minutes
Courtesy of the artists and Nicole Klagsbrun Gallery, New York

Sebastian Bear-McClard and Barney Kulok
River of Shadows: WINDSHIELD
(N 40° 44.401, W-73° 56.837), 2005
Digital video loop; 20:57 minutes
Courtesy of the artists and Nicole Klagsbrun Gallery, New York

Vija Celmins
Alliance, 1982
Three-color aquatint, mezzotint, and drypoint
23 $7/8$ x 19 $3/8$ in.
Courtesy of McKee Gallery, New York

Vija Celmins
Concentric Bearings B, 1985
Two-color aquatint, mezzotint, and drypoint
17 $3/8$ x 14 $1/2$ in.
Courtesy of McKee Gallery, New York

Vija Celmins
Night Sky 1 (Reversed), 2002
Three-color photoetching, aquatint, photogravure, and drypoint
20 $7/8$ x 24 $1/2$ in.
Courtesy of McKee Gallery, New York

Vija Celmins
Strata, 1982
One-color mezzotint, from 25 individual copperplates mounted on a single aluminum plate
29 $1/2$ x 35 $1/2$ in.
Courtesy of McKee Gallery, New York

David Claerbout
Nightscape Lightbox (first), 2002-2003
Black anodized aluminum lightbox, Cibachrome mounted on
Plexiglas with protection layer
49 ¼ x 57 ½ x 7 ⅞ in.
Courtesy of Rennie Collection, Vancouver, Canada

David Claerbout
Nightscape Lightbox (second), 2002-2003
Black anodized aluminum lightbox, Cibachrome mounted on
Plexiglas with protection layer
49 ¼ x 57 ½ x 7 ⅞ in.
Courtesy of Rennie Collection, Vancouver, Canada

David Claerbout
Nightscape Lightbox (fourth), 2002-2003
Black anodized aluminum lightbox, Cibachrome mounted on
Plexiglas with protection layer
49 ¼ x 57 ½ x 7 ⅞ in.
Courtesy of Rennie Collection, Vancouver, Canada

David Claerbout
Nightscape Lightbox (fifth), 2002-2003
Black anodized aluminum lightbox, Cibachrome mounted on
Plexiglas with protection layer
49 ¼ x 57 ½ x 7 ⅞ in.
Courtesy of Rennie Collection, Vancouver, Canada

Jennifer Coates
Blackblood and Twinkle, 2004
Acrylic on canvas
72 x 60 in.
Courtesy of Kinz, Tillou + Feigen, New York

Jennifer Coates
Black Rift, 2006
Acrylic on canvas
24 x 30 in.
Courtesy of Kinz, Tillou + Feigen, New York

Gregory Crewdson
Untitled (penitent girl), 2001-2002
Digital C-print
48 x 60 in.
Collection of Dr. Bernard and JoAnn Kruger, New York

Susan Crile
Charred Earth, 1994
Pumice, charcoal, oil stick, and pastel on paper
38 x 50 in.
Courtesy of the artist

Russell Crotty
Venus Over High Glade, 2006
Ink and watercolor on paper on fiberglass sphere
12 x 12 x 12 in.
Courtesy of the artist and Hosfelt Gallery,
New York and San Francisco

Tim Davis
Bradford Pear from "Illilluminations," 2004
C-print
48 x 60 in.
Courtesy of the artist and
Greenberg Van Doren Gallery, New York

Jen DeNike
What Do You Believe In, 2008
Eighteen black-and-white photographs
8 x 10 in. each
Courtesy of Smith-Stewart, New York

Stan Douglas
Every Building on 100 West Hastings, 2001
C-print
23 ½ x 96 in.
Courtesy of David Zwirner, New York

Juliane Eirich
Beach Chairs, 2004
C-print mounted on Alu-Dibond
36 x 96 in.
Courtesy of Peter Poby, New York

Juliane Eirich
Life Guard House, 2004
C-print mounted on Alu-Dibond
36 x 96 in.
Courtesy of Peter Poby, New York

Spencer Finch
Moonlight (Luna County, New Mexico, July 13, 2003), 2003
Fluorescent bulb and fixture filters
36 x 2 ½ in.
Courtesy of the artist

Spencer Finch
Study for Darkness 4, 2008
Lightbox and filters
16 x 24 in.
Courtesy of the artist

Spencer Finch
Study for Darkness 5, 2008
Lightbox and filters
16 x 24 in.
Courtesy of the artist

Spencer Finch
Study for Darkness 6, 2008
Lightbox and filters
16 x 24 in.
Courtesy of the artist

Ewan Gibbs
London, 2005
Pencil on paper
16 ½ x 23 ⅜ in.
Collection of Glenn Fuhrman, New York
Courtesy of The FLAG Art Foundation, New York

Ewan Gibbs
New York, 2003
Ink on graph paper
11 ¾ x 8 ¼ in.
Collection of Glenn Fuhrman, New York
Courtesy of The FLAG Art Foundation, New York

Susan Graham
Insomnia, 2003/2008
Sugar, egg whites, and scent
Dimensions variable
Courtesy of Schroeder Romero Gallery, New York

Laurent Grasso
Infinite Light, 2006/2008
Neon
Dimensions variable
Courtesy of the artist and Galerie Chez Valentin, Paris

Laurent Grasso
L'éclipse, 2006
DVD projection
Courtesy of Galerie Chez Valentin, Paris

David Hammons
Phat Free, 1995-1999
Videotape transferred to DVD, paper, and paperboard box;
5:02 minutes
Courtesy of Zwirner & Wirth, New York

Todd Hido
1738, 2003
Chromogenic print
24 x 20 in.
Courtesy of Stephen Wirtz Gallery, San Francisco

Todd Hido
2611-A, 2001
Chromogenic print
38 x 30 in.
Courtesy of Stephen Wirtz Gallery, San Francisco

Todd Hido
2552, 1999
Chromogenic print
24 x 20 in.
Courtesy of Stephen Wirtz Gallery, San Francisco

Yvonne Jacquette
Above Times Square, 2003
Oil on canvas
63 x 72 ½ in.
Courtesy of the artist and DC Moore Gallery, New York

Yeon Jin Kim
Dream I, 2008
Single-channel video; 11:29 minutes
Courtesy of the artist

Yeon Jin Kim
Dream II, 2008
Single-channel video; 8:20 minutes
Courtesy of the artist

Yeon Jin Kim
Dream III, 2008
Single-channel video; 8:06 minutes
Courtesy of the artist

Halina Kliem
I Want To See Stars, 2004
Single-channel digital video installation; 2 minutes
Courtesy of DUVE Berlin

Doina Kraal
Sprookjesbos 2, 2005
Painted aluminium tree cut-outs with slide projection
Dimensions variable
Courtesy of the artist and Soledad Senlle Gallery, Amsterdam

Barney Kulok
FDR Baseball Fields, New York NY, 2004
Digital transparency in lightbox
20 x 24 in.
Courtesy of Debevoise & Plimpton LLP

Barney Kulok
Greenpoint Avenue, Brooklyn NY, 2004
Digital transparency in lightbox
20 x 24 in.
Courtesy of Debevoise & Plimpton LLP

Barney Kulok
Purves Street, Queens NY, 2004
Digital transparency in lightbox
20 x 24 in.
Courtesy of the artist and Nicole Klagsbrun Gallery

Barney Kulok
Skillman Avenue, Queens NY, 2004
Digital transparency in lightbox
20 x 24 in.
Courtesy of the artist and Nicole Klagsbrun Gallery

Charles LaBelle
Driftworks – Barcelona (Gothic Quarters, Night), 2005
Compound photograph
27 x 33 in.
Courtesy of Anna Kustera Gallery, New York

Claude Lévêque
La nuit pendant que vous dormez je détruis le monde, 2007
Neon
78 ¾ in. long
Collection of Zadig & Voltaire, Paris.
Courtesy of the artist and Kamel Mennour, Paris

Robert Longo
Horse Head Nebula, 2007
Charcoal on paper
25 x 42 ½ in.
Courtesy of the artist and Metro Pictures, New York

Britta Lumer
Nachtstadt / City at Night II, 2006
Indian ink on Ingres paper
19 ¾ x 25 ⅖ in.
Courtesy of the artist and Galerie Morgen, Berlin

Britta Lumer
Nachtstadt / City at Night III, 2006
Indian ink on Ingres paper
19 ¾ x 25 ⅖ in.
Courtesy of the artist and Galerie Morgen, Berlin

Britta Lumer
Nachtstadt / City at Night IV, 2006
Indian ink on Ingres paper
19 ¾ x 25 ⅖ in.
Courtesy of the artist and Galerie Morgen, Berlin

Vera Lutter
30th Street Station, Philadelphia, II: April 17, 2006, 2006
Silver gelatin print
31 ½ x 57 ½ in.
© Vera Lutter. Courtesy of Gagosian Gallery, New York

Florian Maier-Aichen
Untitled, 2005
C-print
69 ¾ x 92 ½ in.
Collection of David and Kim Schrader

Vik Muniz
Viewing from Guanahani, Bahamas from "Pictures of Air," 2001
C-print
60 x 48 in.
Courtesy of the artist and Sikkema Jenkins & Co., New York

Lauren Orchowski
Little Rocket, Starry Night, 2007
Wood, metal, polymer, photographic paper, and fluorescent bulb
24 ¼ x 30 x 23 in.
Courtesy of the artist

Lauren Orchowski
Rocket and Twist, 2007
Wood, metal, rubber, photographic paper, and fluorescent bulb
24 ½ x 30 x 23 in.
Courtesy of the artist

John Pilson
Dark Empire, 2003
Single-channel video
Approx. 25 minutes
Courtesy of the artist and Nicole Klagsbrun Gallery, New York

Thomas Ruff
Nacht 2 I, 1992
C-print
7 7/8 x 8 1/4 in.
Courtesy of the artist and David Zwirner, New York

Thomas Ruff
Nacht 4 II, 1992
C-print
7 7/8 x 8 1/4 in.
Courtesy of the artist and David Zwirner, New York

Thomas Ruff
Nacht 17 I, 1992
C-print
7 7/8 x 8 1/4 in.
Courtesy of the artist and David Zwirner, New York

Thomas Ruff
Nacht 18 I, 1994
C-print
7 7/8 x 8 1/4 in.
Courtesy of the artist and David Zwirner, New York

Thomas Ruff
Stern 17h 51m/-22°, 1990
C-print
102 3/8 x 74 in.
Private collection, New Jersey

Pat Steir
Starry Night, 2000
Photogravure, aquatint, and pochoir
28 7/8 x 25 3/8 in.
Courtesy of Pace Prints, New York

Deborah Stratman
In Order Not To Be Here, 2002
Video transfer from 16mm film; 33 minutes
Courtesy of the artist

Marc Swanson
Boy in Tree, 2005
Glass, enamel, and glitter
36 x 24 in.
Private collection, New Jersey

Marc Swanson
Nests, 2005
Glass, enamel, and glitter
36 x 24 in.
Collection of Arthur and Connie Zeckendorf, New York

Marc Swanson and Neil Gust
Love is all Around, 2007
Video; 3:51 minutes
Courtesy of the artists and Bellwether, New York

Susanna Thornton
Forest/Lights I from "NIGHTSTILLS," 2004
Color photographic C-print mounted on Plexiglas
40 x 50 in.
Courtesy of the artist

Susanna Thornton
Nightstill I from "NIGHTSTILLS," 2004
Color photographic C-print mounted on Plexiglas
40 x 40 in.
Courtesy of the artist

Susanna Thornton
Nightstill II from "NIGHTSTILLS," 2004
Color photographic C-print mounted on Plexiglas
40 x 40 in.
Courtesy of the artist

Susanna Thornton
Rainbow/Shadow from "NIGHTSTILLS," 2004
Color photographic C-print mounted on Plexiglas
40 x 50 in.
Courtesy of the artist

Jeff Wall
After "Spring Snow" by Yukio Mishima, chapter 34, 2004
C-print
25 1/2 x 29 in.
Courtesy of Marian Goodman Gallery, New York

Andy Warhol
Sleep, 1963
16mm black-and-white silent film; 5 hours and 21 minutes
© 2008 The Andy Warhol Museum, Pittsburgh, Pa.,
a museum of Carnegie Institute

Thomas Weaver
Morning After Curtain, 2008
Acrylic on paper
48 x 60 in.
Courtesy of the artist

Shizuka Yokomizo
Stranger (10), 1999
C-print
50 x 42 ½ in.
Courtesy of the artist

Shizuka Yokomizo
Stranger (13), 2000
C-print
50 x 42 ½ in.
Courtesy of the artist

Shizuka Yokomizo
Stranger (17), 2000
C-print
50 x 42 ½ in.
Courtesy of the artist

Kohei Yoshiyuki
Untitled, 1971
Gelatin silver print
20 x 24 in.
©Kohei Yoshiyuki. Courtesy of Yossi Milo Gallery, New York

Kohei Yoshiyuki
Untitled, 1971
Gelatin silver print
20 x 24 in.
©Kohei Yoshiyuki. Courtesy of Yossi Milo Gallery, New York

Kohei Yoshiyuki
Untitled, 1973
Gelatin silver print
20 x 24 in.
©Kohei Yoshiyuki. Courtesy of Yossi Milo Gallery, New York

Kohei Yoshiyuki
Untitled, 1973
Gelatin silver print
20 x 24 in.
©Kohei Yoshiyuki. Courtesy of Yossi Milo Gallery, New York

John Zurier
Night 15, 2007
Distemper on linen
30 x 20 in.
Courtesy of the artist

John Zurier
Night 16, 2007
Distemper on linen
30 x 20 in.
Courtesy of the artist

John Zurier
Night 30, 2008
Distemper on linen
30 x 20 in.
Courtesy of the artist and Larry Becker Contemporary Art,
Philadelphia

John Zurier
Night 31, 2008
Distemper on linen
30 x 20 in.
Courtesy of the artist and Larry Becker Contemporary Art,
Philadelphia

THE FRIENDS OF THE HUNTER COLLEGE ART GALLERIES

Helen Schectman
Eli A. Schwartz
Barbara A. Scott
Shirley E. Scott
Edith Shapiro
Judith Siegel
Richard Stapleford
Elinor Stevens
Melville Straus
Annette and Robert Swain
Dianne Wallace and Lowell M. Schulman
Ann Sloven
Joanne Kesten Weinberg
Isabel Wilcox
Jacqueline G. Wilson
Brian W. Wood

NON-RESIDENT FRIENDS
Barbara Berkman
Roslyn Levin

ASSOCIATE MEMBERS
Millie Benson
Stanley Blum
Julia Boddewyn
Michael Brennan
Diana Cooper
Josephine Demarest
Barbra Fitzgerald
Deborah Garwood
Mamie Gerardi
Phyllis Glantz
Roslyn Goldstein
L. Michael Griffel
Lynne Harlow
Gabriele Hoffmann
Siochain Hughes
Barbara F. Johnston
Joanne L. Kesten
Lynda Klich
Tim Laun
Bernice Leibowitz
Leanne T. Martinson
Renee G. Mayer
Robin Moore
Guna S. Mundheim
James O'Connor
Dorothy Oravec
Marisa Osorio
Thomas Pihl
Lynn Sullivan
Rosemarie Tishelman

Lisa Vergara
Virginia Waldie
Joanne Kester Weinberg

CORPORATE/FOUNDATIONS
The Heisman Trophy Trust
Wolf Kahn and Emily Mason Foundation

HUNTER COLLEGE OF THE CITY UNIVERSITY OF NEW YORK
Jennifer J. Raab, President
Vita Rabinowitz, Provost and Vice President for Academic Affairs
Shirley Clay Scott, Dean, School of Arts and Sciences
Thomas Weaver, Chair of the Department of Art

THE HUNTER COLLEGE ART GALLERIES
Thomas Weaver, Executive Director
Joachim Pissarro, Bershad Professor of Art History and Director
Tracy L. Adler, Curator
Mara Hoberman, Curator
Julia Moreno, Curatorial Assistant
Phi Nguyen, Preparator
Tim Laun, MFA Building Studio Manager

THE BERTHA AND KARL LEUBSDORF ART GALLERY
Located in the Hunter West Building at the southwest corner of
68th Street and Lexington Avenue
Hours: Tuesday through Saturday from 1 to 6 pm.
Information: (212) 772 – 4991

HUNTER COLLEGE/TIMES SQUARE GALLERY
450 West 41st Street between 9th and 10th Avenue
Hours: Tuesday through Saturday from 1 to 6 pm.
Information: (212) 772 – 4991

PHOTO CREDITS:
Page 17: ©The Metropolitan Museum of Art
Plate VIII: Photograph by Monica Ruzansky
Plate IX and XXVIII: © Thomas Ruff
Plate X: Published by Pace Editions, Inc.
Plate XVII: © Britta Lumer
Plate XXIII: © Juliane Eirich
Plate XXVI: Courtesy of the artist and Luhring Augustine, New York

COLOPHON
This book was designed by {c/c}
Edited by Casey Ruble
Printing by Lancaster Reprographics
Edition of 2,500

ISBN 1-885998-81-3